THE
POCKET
Pride

Published in 2025
by Gemini Books
Part of Gemini Books Group
Based in Woodbridge and London

Marine House, Tide Mill Way,
Woodbridge, Suffolk IP12 1AP
United Kingdom
www.geminibooks.com

Text and Design © 2025 Gemini Adult Books Ltd
Part of the Gemini Pockets series

Cover image: Shutterstock Ltd/Michael Derrer Fuchs
Text by Michael Rosner

ISBN 978-1-80247-298-1

Manufacturer's EU Representative: Eurolink Compliance Limited, 25 Herbert
Place, Dublin, D02 AY86, Republic of Ireland. admin@eurolink-europe.ie

Printed in Poland

10 9 8 7 6 5 4 3 2 1

Contents

Introduction

Pride is a celebration, a protest, a party, a riot. It's individual and it's about the community, it's personal and it's public. Pride can mean a lot of different things but at its core Pride marks the struggle for LGBTQIA+ people to gain equality in the world. Pride evokes feelings of self-love, happiness and the inclusion of others in the face of oppression.

When LGBTQIA+ people demanded equal rights, they began to become more visible as a community and were no longer confined to the shadows and closets. They were able to finally stand proud of who they were. Pride marches, and the people, organizations and symbols that helped shaped them, are a key part of providing visibility to LGBTQIA+ communities across the globe and highlighting the issues they face.

In this book you will discover some of the key moments and people involved in the pursuit of equal rights for LGBTQIA+ people. Along the way, you will be inspired by LGBTQIA+ individuals from around the world showing us the importance of self-acceptance and the beauty we can find within ourselves.

66 There will not be a magic day when we wake up and it's now okay to express ourselves publicly. We make that day by doing things publicly until it's simply the way things are. 99

TAMMY BALDWIN, US SENATOR FOR WISCONSIN, POSTING ON X, 26 APRIL 2024

Chapter One

Rebellions & Rights

What is Pride for?

A lot of the messaging of the Pride movement can be linked to self-love. For a long time, LGBTQIA+ people were made to feel like they had to hide their identity, for fear of discrimination and punishment. By projecting a message of loving yourself, and accepting who you are, the movement hopes to inspire people who are experiencing similar feelings of fear and uncertainty to unite.

Another important facet of the movement is the demand to be treated equally to heterosexuals. Many of the rights and freedoms of LGBTQIA+ people in the 21st century are directly linked to the campaigns, protests and actions begun by influential figures and groups of the 20th century and there are numerous individuals and organizations that continue that legacy to this day.

"If you can't love yourself, how in the hell are you going to love somebody else?"

RUPAUL CHARLES,
DRAG QUEEN AND TELEVISION HOST

History

The history of LGBTQIA+ people goes back for centuries, and with it their struggle for equality. You can find evidence of same-sex relationships in Mesolithic and Neolithic cave art, ancient Greek philosophy, Latin love poetry and Chinese historical records. Quite simply, there seems to be some form of evidence throughout the history of many cultures around the world. Yet perhaps the most enduring proof of the continued existence of LGBTQIA+ people is in the laws enacted to punish them.

In 1994, LGBT History Month was started in the US by Missouri high-school history teacher Rodney Wilson to highlight the history of gay rights and related civil rights movements. It is celebrated during October in the US to coincide with National Coming Out Day on 11 October.

Persecution

Unfortunately, LGBTQIA+ people have faced persecution throughout history. Imperialism and colonialism have used religious interpretation to justify homophobic laws that punish same-sex relationships, but there are also many secular laws through history that forbade same-sex relationships with punishments as extreme as the death penalty. The 20th century was a time when there were great injustices, but also the beginning of change.

" Every gay and lesbian person who has been lucky enough to survive the turmoil of growing up is a survivor. "

BOB PARIS, ACTOR AND BODYBUILDER

Rights in the USA

Because rights were governed by individual States, some parts of the US achieved progress toward equal rights, while LGBTQIA+ people in other parts of the country were extremely oppressed.

Despite this, crucial efforts toward gaining LGBTQIA+ rights can be traced back to the 1960s. An event that took place on a summer evening in New York City would inspire a movement around the world, demanding equality for all.

The Stonewall Inn

On Christopher Street in Greenwich Village, New York, in the 1960s, there was a tavern called the Stonewall Inn that held the status as a safe place for patrons to be open in their sexuality and gender identity, despite regular police raids.

The inn was popular among the most marginalized people in the community, from drag queens and hustlers to the transgender community, a common target for prejudice and the authorities.

The Stonewall Uprising

In the early morning of 28 June 1969, during yet another police raid, the Stonewall patrons, long frustrated by police brutality and after the beating and arrest of several gay men and women, gathered outside the bar. As more patrol vehicles arrived, they began shouting at the officers: "Gay Power!" "We shall overcome!" People started throwing pennies and empty beer bottles at police vehicles. Three nights of unrest followed, and the event marked a new beginning for gay rights in the USA and around the world.

"When we came back on Saturday night, we stood there on the street and held hands and kissed – something we would never have done three days earlier. It made me feel wonderful. I stood there with chills."

MICHAEL LEVINE, STONEWALL INN PATRON, ANTI-DEFAMATION LEAGUE INTERVIEW, 2011

The Stonewall Riots

The Stonewall riots, as they came to be known, gained a mythological status in the LGBTQIA+ community and ultimately inspired the formation of an organized effort to gain visibility and rights.

Stormé DeLarverie, a drag-king performer and lesbian woman, is widely recounted as being the first to physically resist the police.

"It was a rebellion, it was an uprising. It wasn't no damn riot."

STORMÉ DELARVERIE,
WWW.STORME-DELARVERIE.COM

66 Stonewall represented, absolutely, the first time that the LGBT community successfully fought back and forged an organized movement and community. 99

MARK SEGAL,
FOUNDING MEMBER OF GAY LIBERATION FRONT

Gay Liberation Front

Following the events of the Stonewall Uprising, the creation of the Gay Liberation Front soon followed. While the Gay Liberation Front was not the first LGBTQIA+ organization in US history, it was the first to explicitly signal its purpose by using the word "gay" in its name. Earlier groups were seen as being too weak and mild in their approach to gaining rights, unlike the revolutionary Gay Liberation Front which was born from the flames of Stonewall.

" Gay Liberation changed the methodology. We emphasized self-acceptance, fighting back, and creating community. That, for gay people, was a revolutionary act, a revolutionary event. Troy Perry creating a gay-friendly church was a revolutionary act… 1969, 1970 and 1971 was a period of revolution for gay people, and this revolution is still needed today. "

DR DONALD KHILHEFNER, EARLY MEMBER OF GLF, INTERVIEW WITH THE LGBTQ HISTORY PROJECT

The Fight for Rights

The Gay Liberation Front sometimes engaged in provocative activism and disruption to bring attention to the struggle for equality, taking inspiration from the anti-war and civil rights movements.

In addition to staging sit-ins and organizing protests, a crucial role the Gay Liberation Front played was to encourage open dialogue between the different factions of the LGBTQIA+ community.

The Flame Spreads

The nature of the Gay Liberation Front as a coalition meant that multiple splinter groups formed from the different factions. This enabled a greater focus on issues facing groups like lesbians, transgender people and people of colour, but eventually led to the abandonment of the Gay Liberation Front.

Cooper Do-Nuts

Even before Stonewall, however, there was an uprising in reaction to police harassment of LGBTQIA+ people at a 24-hour doughnut café in LA.

According to John Rechy, the author of the gay culture novel *City of Night* (1963), this occurred ten years before, in 1959.

Radicalesbians

A group of women, including Martha Shelley, Lois Hart and Ellen Broidy, went on to form the Radicalesbians, an organization for the advancement of lesbian rights.

This group would demonstrate against the lack of lesbian women in other women-led movements, memorably at a conference by the National Organization for Women (NOW), a leading feminist group in the US.

Radicalesbians would go on to represent a key faction in the feminist movement overall, especially during its second wave, by giving lesbians a voice in the fight for gender equality.

" I have met many, many feminists who were not Lesbians but I have never met a Lesbian who was not a feminist. "

MARTHA SHELLEY,
'NOTES OF A RADICAL LESBIAN', 1969

Street Transvestite Action Revolutionaries

The gender non-conforming individuals from the original Gay Liberation Front went on to found Street Transvestite Action Revolutionaries (STAR) in 1970, with Sylvia Rivera and Marsha P. Johnson, both famous drag queens throughout New York City, taking the reins.

Some of STAR's core actions included campaigning on behalf of homeless gay youth and for the rights of gay prisoners; it was considered a groundbreaking group in the gay rights movement.

" REVOLUTION NOW!
Give me a G!
Give me an A!
Give me a Y!
Give me a P!
Give me an O!
Give me a W!
Give me an E!
Give me an R!
GAY POWER!
Louder!
GAY POWER! "

SYLVIA RIVERA,
AS CITED IN RHETORIC REVIEW, 2017

Third World Gay Revolution

Another group that formed after the dissolution of the Gay Liberation Front, the Third World Gay Revolution consisted of Black and Latino members, such as poet Néstor Latrónico and graphic artist Juan Carlos Vidal who presented a 16-point manifesto that highlighted the triple-discriminations they faced: homophobia, racism and classism. They laid the groundwork for the continued recognition of the unique issues faced by LGBTQIA+ people of colour.

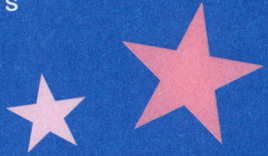

" **We want the right of self-determination over the use of our bodies: The right to be gay, anytime, anyplace… The right to free dress and adornment.** "

THE SIXTEEN POINT PLATFORM AND PROGRAM, DRAFTED 11 NOVEMBER 1970

Gay Activists Alliance

Several members leaving the Gay Liberation Front would go on to form the Gay Activists Alliance (GAA), intending to focus solely on issues relating to LGBTQIA+ rights and seeking to distance themselves from far-left radical politics.

The group believed that there was more to gain from being politically neutral, seeking to engage all sides of the political spectrum.

"Before the public conscience, we demand an immediate end to all oppression of homosexuals and the immediate unconditional recognition of these basic rights: the right to our own feelings… the right to love… the right to our own bodies… [and] the right to be persons."

PREAMBLE TO THE CONSTITUTION OF GAY
ACTIVISTS ALLIANCE OF NEW YORK

Zaps

Alongside protests and pressing for legislation, the Gay Activists Alliance became renowned for its use of "zaps", although they were not the first group to do this. Described by GAA member Arthur Bell as "political theater for educating the gay masses", the "zaps" were lighthearted in nature and normally involved some form of sit-in and an effort to create public embarrassment, although at times they could also involve violent altercations and property damage.

Government Roles

As LGBTQIA+ communities gained visibility, from marching in the streets to serving their communities, individuals began to be elected into government roles locally and nationally. This enabled them to propose legislations that gave protections to LGBTQIA+ people.

Kathy Kozachenko made history as the first openly gay person elected to political office in the USA when she was appointed to Michigan's Ann Arbor City Council in 1974. Less than a year later, Elaine Noble was elected to the Massachusetts House of Representatives.

Don't Ask, Don't Tell

The freedom to serve in the military is a right that LGBTQIA+ people can be routinely denied. Don't Ask, Don't Tell was the policy of the US Army in relation to this and forbade openly LGBTQIA+ Americans from serving in their army. It was brought into law in 1993 by Bill Clinton and repealed in 2010 by Barack Obama.

Section 28

Aside from laws which make being LGBTQIA+ illegal, there are also laws that aim to restrict the ability for members to live as their authentic selves. One such example is Section 28 which was introduced by the British Parliament under Margaret Thatcher in 1988.

This set of legislature aimed to outlaw the "promotion of homosexuality", particularly in education, and resulted in protests. Section 28 was completely repealed across the UK by 2003.

Marriage Equality

As of 2024, same-sex marriage was legal in 36 UN Member States, the result of tireless activism by many of those countries' LGBTQIA+ communities. This is in contrast to 35 UN Member States that have banned same-sex marriage at a constitutional level.

LGBTQIA+ Criminalization

In 2024, there are 62 UN Member States that criminalize LGBTQIA+ people, including seven UN Member States where being LGBTQIA+ is punishable by death. Pride began as a reaction to discrimination and this ongoing threat is the reason why Pride continues to be important, a reminder of the battles won and the battles still being fought.

Chapter Two

The First Pride Marches

The First Anniversary of Stonewall

The Eastern Regional Conference of Homophile Organizations held yearly pickets after 1962 to promote the rights of the LGBTQIA+ community.

In 1970, the focus of the pickets was redirected toward a tribute to the Stonewall Uprising. The name Christopher Street Liberation Day was adopted, in reference to the location of the Stonewall Inn, and thus the first Pride march was conceived to take place on the last weekend in June.

" We wrote a statement to change the annual Independence Hall demonstration into a full-blown march, honoring what had happened at Stonewall and what we hoped would happen moving forward. "

ELLEN BROIDY, RECALLING THE IDEA FOR THE FIRST PRIDE MARCH, INTERVIEW WITH THE LGBTQ HISTORY PROJECT

Preparing for Pride

Plans began in New York, Los Angeles and Chicago to mark the last weekend in June with a march through the cities. The mood was to be jovial and positive.

Despite being traumatic for its participants, the Stonewall Uprising was a moment of empowerment and liberation and the organizers wanted the march to reflect this. It was to be a demonstration but also a celebration.

The Last Weekend in June

When the momentous weekend arrived, thousands paraded through the streets of New York, Los Angeles and Chicago. Many were waving banners or holding signs with slogans such as "Gay Pride" or "Gay and Proud".

Many residents came out to see what all the noise and commotion was about, some looking on with shock and disgust but others with admiration and respect. The inaugural Christopher Street Liberation Day was a resounding success, and the idea became an annual event.

The Messages of Pride

Over the years, Pride has refocused as new issues affect the LGBTQIA+ community. Toward the end of the 20th century, campaigns for those suffering from AIDS were at the forefront and awareness around HIV/AIDS continues to be a part of Pride.

While there are still important political and social issues to be raised at Prides around the world, they are also a time of great happiness and festivity. Bright colours, fun music and people dancing in the streets are all commonplace at a Pride event. In 2024, Pride events took place in over 30 major US cities or metropolitan areas and they continue to grow and spread around the world.

" I feel anger, frustration, hope, joy, grief, pride, empowerment and love. I feel all of these and more because I can't talk about HIV without talking about a whole host of other issues like racism, homophobia, sexism, poverty and others. "

REGGIE WILLIAMS, AIDS ACTIVIST, FIRST EXECUTIVE DIRECTOR OF THE NATIONAL TASK FORCE ON AIDS PREVENTION

UK Gay Liberation Front

Inspired by the work of the Gay Liberation Front, two students – Bob Mellors and Aubrey Walter – formed the British chapter of the group in October 1970, creating an international movement that extended across the Atlantic.

The group, like its American counterpart, engaged in radical and provocative activism, notably protesting against the Nationwide Festival of Light which they viewed as a homophobic organization that used religion as an excuse to discriminate against LGBTQIA+ people.

London Pride

The first Pride march in the UK happened in London on 1 July 1972. The British chapter of the Gay Liberation Front and the Campaign for Homosexual Equality were the main organizers of this historic event. The date was chosen by finding the closest Saturday to the anniversary of the Stonewall Uprising, a tradition that many other international LGBTQIA+ groups have used when initiating Pride marches.

Kissing in the Park

The first British Pride march was heavily monitored throughout by the police who launched verbal tirades at the participants. A public kiss-in was held in protest at public decency laws which made same-sex kissing illegal. By this point there were simply too many gay men kissing each other and too few police to make any arrests.

While New York is the origination of the political movement and has the USA's largest Pride march, with about 2.5 million attendees, Toronto hosts over 3 million and Sau Paulo 4 million. About 1.5 million attend London Pride.

British Campaigns

The British Gay Liberation Front would eventually disband in 1973 but many rights groups would be established and former members, such as Peter Tatchell and Simon Warner, continued campaigning, employing similar tactics to bring attention to LGBTQIA+ rights.

" GLF was a glorious, enthusiastic and often chaotic mix of anarchists, hippies, leftwingers, feminists, liberals and counter-culturalists. Despite our differences, we shared a radical idealism – a dream of what the world could and should be – free from not just homophobia but the whole sex-shame culture. "

PETER TATCHELL, *GUARDIAN*, 2010

Chapter Three

Icons of Pride

Honour for Individuals

The Pride movement thrives because of the meaningful contributions LGBTQIA+ people have made and continue to make toward equal rights for their community. All around the world, courageous individuals overcome adversity to help shape their future for the better.

Honouring the queer ancestors who helped pave the way for future generations has become a key feature of Pride as it has grown. There are too many to count, but you will find a few trailblazers in the following pages.

" We will not win our rights by staying quietly in our closets… we are coming out! "

HARVEY MILK, FROM HIS HOPE SPEECH AT GAY FREEDOM DAY, SAN FRANCISCO, 25 JUNE 1978

Alan Turing (1912–54)

Alan Turing was an English codebreaker who played a crucial role in the victory of many battles fought by the Allied powers. Despite his importance to the war effort, in 1952 he was found guilty of "homosexual acts" and was chemically castrated as an alternative punishment to prison time.

Tragically, Alan Turing took his own life in 1954, but the legacy he left behind led many people to pursue justice on his behalf.

The Alan Turing Law

Alan Turing received an official pardon for his "crimes" by Queen Elizabeth II in 2013. The pardoning led the way for the introduction of the so-called "Alan Turing Law" which allowed for the pardoning of all people convicted of "homosexual activity". This included renowned Irish playwright Oscar Wilde who was convicted of the same crime in 1895. Another 49,000 other people were also pardoned.

James Baldwin (1924–87)

The African-American writer explored themes of sexuality, race, class and masculinity in his novels, which influenced both the civil rights and gay liberation movements. His works feature gay and bisexual men, often looking for self- and social acceptance.

"Love him and let him love you. Do you think anything else under heaven really matters?"

JAMES BALDWIN,
GIOVANNI'S ROOM (1956)

Allan Horsfall (1927–2012)

"The grandfather of the gay rights movement" was the moniker earned by Allan Horsfall due to his efforts in the UK before homosexuality was decriminalized. He began raising attention to the plight of LGBTQIA+ Britons as early as 1964, five years before Stonewall. He was part of a group that founded the Campaign for Homosexual Equality which during its operations would become the largest LGBTQIA+ group in the UK.

George Hislop (1927–2005)

A prominent figure in the history of LGBTQIA+ rights in Canada, George Hislop was involved in the creation of the Community Homophile Association of Toronto, and helped oversee Canada's first gay rights protest in 1971. He was particularly successful in campaigning for the rights of same-sex partners to receive the same pension benefits given to their heterosexual peers.

Harvey Milk (1930–78)

The first openly gay politician elected in the state of California, Harvey Milk was an inspiring activist for the LGBTQIA+ community, valuing unity and the benefits of positive neighbourhood relations. On 27 November 1978, he was tragically assassinated less than a year into his election term, alongside San Francisco mayor George Moscone. Many view him as a martyr because of the circumstances surrounding his death, a huge loss to the gay rights movement.

" It takes no compromise to give people their rights … it takes no money to respect the individual. It takes no political deal to give people freedom. It takes no survey to remove repression. "

HARVEY MILK

The Mayor of Castro Street

Milk owned a camera shop in Castro Street, San Francisco. He became such a prominent figure in the gay scene of the area that he earned the name the Mayor of Castro Street. He formed the Castro Village Association to create a coalition of fellow gay business owners, forming an alliance with the Teamsters Union.

Posthumous Awards

In 2009, Harvey Milk was posthumously awarded the Presidential Medal of Freedom by President Barack Obama. In November 2021, the US Navy launched the USNS Harvey Milk, a John Lewis-class fleet oiler. It was the first US Navy vessel to be named for an openly gay person.

Barbara Gittings

(1932–2007)

As a pioneering activist for gay rights pre-Stonewall and after, Gittings challenged the classification of homosexuality as a mental illness, set up Daughters of Bilitis, the first lesbian civil rights group in the US, and campaigned for gay literature in libraries.

" I've had the satisfaction of working with other gay people all across the country to get the bigots off our backs, to oil the closet door hinges, to change prejudiced hearts and minds, and to show that gay love is good for us and for the rest of the world too. "

BARBARA GITTINGS, 1999

Audre Lorde (1934–92)

The Black lesbian poet and feminist dedicated her life and talents to confronting injustices. Her work dealt with issues related to civil rights, feminism, lesbianism, illness, disability, race, patriarchy and the exploration of Black female identity. A self-described "black, lesbian, mother, warrior, poet", she was known for her bold and powerful language.

"You do not have to be me in order for us to fight alongside each other. I do not have to be you to recognize that our wars are the same."

AUDRE LORDE, *SISTER OUTSIDER* (1984)

Larry Kramer (1935–2020)

A playwright, film producer, author, activist and fierce advocate, Kramer's work was pivotal in the fight against AIDS and for LGBTQIA+ rights.

He co-founded the Gay Men's Health Crisis (GMHC) and the AIDS Coalition to Unleash Power (ACT).

Angela Davis (1944–)

A political activist and academic, Davis is an outspoken advocate for LGBTQIA+ rights. Her approach to activism focuses on the interconnected struggles of sexism, racism and homophobia.

She was an honorary co-chair of the Women's March on Washington in January 2017.

Marsha P. Johnson (1945–92)

Affectionately called Saint Marsha, Johnson was a figurehead of her community known for her involvement in the Stonewall Uprising. She fought tirelessly for the advancement of LGBTQIA+ rights, in particular those of homeless youth as she regularly experienced homelessness herself.

Her untimely passing in 1992 was ruled a suicide by the police, yet close friends continue to search for answers, believing foul play could have been involved.

"Darling, I want my gay rights now. I think it's about time the gay brothers and sisters got their rights ... especially the women."

MARSHA P. JOHNSON

Sylvia Rivera
(1951–2002)

Like Marsha P. Johnson, Sylvia Rivera was an activist working to promote the rights of the gender non-conforming community. She was renowned for her speeches outlining the need for gay rights and the struggles facing the transgender community. Just a few months before she passed away in 2002, the final bill of an anti-discrimination law in New York she helped to introduce was passed, showing how Sylvia worked tirelessly for her community until her last moments.

Georgina Beyer (1957–2023)

In 1999, Georgina Beyer, a New Zealand woman of European and Māori descent, became the world's first openly transgender member of parliament when she was elected to serve the electorate of Wairarapa. During her time in the New Zealand parliament she supported both the introduction of civil unions for LGBTQIA+ couples and bills ensuring sexuality was a protected characteristic under anti-discrimination laws.

RuPaul Charles (1960–)

The actor, television host, singer, producer, writer and drag queen and 11-time Emmy award-winner revolutionized the media representation of drag culture with his reality TV show RuPaul's Drag Race, launched in 2009. He uses his platform to discuss topics like inclusion, equality, female empowerment and racial discrimination; he is an activist for voter registration for the LGBTQIA+ community.

Laverne Cox (1972–)

Actress and LGBTQIA+ activist, Cox is a trailblazer for trans rights. She was the first openly transgender person to be nominated for a Primetime Emmy Award for her performance in the Netflix series *Orange is the New Black*.

Elliot Page (1987–)

Canadian actor, producer and activist Page has spoken out against discriminatory legislation toward the trans community and is a vocal advocate for LGBTQIA+ rights. He came out as a trans man in 2020.

"We deserve to experience love fully, equally, without shame and without compromise."

ELLIOT PAGE, FROM HIS SPEECH AT HRCF'S TIME TO THRIVE CONFERENCE, 14 FEBRUARY 2014

Symbols of Pride

Symbology plays an important role in LGBTQIA+ culture. In periods of history where same-sex activity was illegal, LGBTQIA+ people used non-verbal cues such as clothing to help identify each other. The Pride movement makes use of emblems and also a large array of flags to provide visibility to the causes they represent.

Pink Triangle

Originally used by the Nazis to identify gay men, the pink triangle began to be reappropriated by the LGBTQIA+ community in the 1970s as a memorial to the victims of Nazi persecution. It found particular prominence during AIDS activism in the late 1980s.

The OG Flag

One of the most identifiable symbols of the Pride movement are the flags that create a dazzling array of colour, serving as emblems to unite the communities they represent. The rainbow flag stands out as the most recognizable of these flags, itself having gone through different variations which all continue to be flown today.

The original rainbow flag was designed by US Army veteran Gilbert Baker in June 1978. It was a meeting with Harvey Milk that helped inspire him to create the iconic flag, a rallying banner for his community. Eight colours came together to produce the flag, with each reflecting a specific meaning: violet symbolized spirit; indigo symbolized serenity; turquoise symbolized magic; green, nature; yellow, sunlight; orange, healing; red, life; and hot pink, sex.

66 What I liked about the rainbow is that it fits all of us. It's all the colors. It represents all the genders. It represents all the races. It's the rainbow of humanity. 99

GILBERT BAKER, GILBERTBAKER.COM

Dropping the Pink

After Harvey Milk was assassinated in November 1978, many members of the LGBTQIA+ community used rainbow flags to visibly show their support for him and the rights he was fighting for. This increase in demand led to the hot pink colour being dropped, as that fabric was harder to source. This led to the first variation of the flag, now with only seven colours.

The Current Flag

In 1979 the flag was changed by Baker yet again, this time replacing the turquoise and indigo stripes with blue. It is this incarnation that remains one of the most prominent symbols of the Pride movement and of the LGBTQIA+ community itself. A powerful signifier for acceptance of the LGBTQIA+ community, it can be seen flying proudly across many cities around the world, particularly during Pride celebrations.

A More Inclusive Flag

The city of Philadelphia introduced a new variation of the rainbow flag in 2017, this time including a brown and a black stripe to raise attention to the issues facing People of Colour within the LGBTQIA+ community. This idea was met with some criticism because the original flag was designed to be inclusive of all races, however it was also praised.

" We should indeed keep calm in the face of difference, and live our lives in a state of inclusion and wonder at the diversity of humanity. "

GEORGE TAKEI, *LIONS AND TIGERS AND BEARS* (2013)

A New Version

The Intersex-Inclusive Progress Pride flag was introduced in 2021 to promote a more inclusive community by adding a chevron with colours and symbols symbolizing LGBTQIA+ people of colour, the trans community and the intersex community. It was designed by Valentino Vecchietti from Intersex Equality Rights UK.

Bisexual Pride

Designed by Michael Page and unveiled in December 1998, the Bisexual flag consists of pink, purple and blue stripes. Page describes the colours as being representations of the bisexual experience. The pink is the attraction to the same sex, while the blue shows the attraction to the opposite sex; the purple in the middle shows the confluence of the two.

❝Remember, bisexuality doesn't mean halfway between gay or straight. It is its own identity.❞

EVAN RACHEL WOOD, TWITTER, 17 SEPTEMBER 2015

Transgender Pride

The Transgender flag was designed by US Army veteran Monica Helms and features five stripes, in baby blue, baby pink and white. Monica was inspired by her friend Michael Page and his creation of the bisexual flag as a way to showcase the pride she felt in being transgender.

Representing colours traditionally associated with gender, blue and pink, the flag also includes white for those who don't associate with either gender.

"We are not what other people say we are. We are who we know ourselves to be, and we are what we love. That's okay."

LAVERNE COX, INTERVIEW IN *ROOKIE*, JULY 2014

Chapter Four

Pride
Around the
World

Inclusion & Acceptance

Pride continues to inspire millions of people around the world to march and promote inclusion and acceptance. Every year, a new pride parade is held in a city for the first time, providing more regional access to Pride events, which in the past were limited to capital cities and large metropolitan centres.

Pride marches are not a franchise. There is no copy-and-paste formula that creates a Pride event. Instead, they are created from the coming together of community and a desire for their voices to be heard. There are still countries which are yet to host a Pride parade despite same-sex activity being legal, but here's a look at some of the record-breaking Pride events held since the inaugural marches.

"I believe that telling our stories, first to ourselves and then to one another and the world, is a revolutionary act."

JANET MOCK, *REDEFINING REALNESS* (2014)

Pride in North America

Like the first Pride marches held in the USA in June 1970, many cities and organizations choose a date on or near the anniversary of the Stonewall Uprising, as recognition of the efforts of those to pave the way for future generations. The first march north of the border was during 1978 in Vancouver, although rights demonstrations had been organized by the group Gay Alliance Toward Equality as early as 1973.

Pride in the UK

The first Pride march was held in London on 1 July 1972, but many individual and diverse Pride events occur regionally – over 180 events a year.

One of the biggest and most popular is the Brighton & Hove Pride Festival, held in the first week of August.

Pride in Europe

Münster, Germany became the location for the first Pride event held in Europe on 29 April 1972. Paris, France, the city of love, hosted its first Pride event on 25 June 1977 and the first Pride event held in Spain occurred a day later on 26 June 1977 in Barcelona. However the Barcelona parade was violently attacked by the police.

Madrid Pride, also known as Madrid Orgullo (MADO), is the biggest Pride parade in Europe, drawing one of the largest crowds (1.5 million) in the world during its week of festivities.

Pride in Oceania

April 1972 would see the first Pride march held in the Southern Hemisphere. Auckland, New Zealand, hosted a "Gay Day" which served as a protest and helped to bring the New Zealand LGBTQIA+ community together. Sydney hosted Australia's first Pride event, styled as Mardi Gras, on 24 June 1978 in solidarity with LGBTQIA+ organizations around the world; it was, however, met with brutal oppression by the police which led to many arrests.

" Never give up. Never, never give up. And know that… ahakoa he te ao wairua – even though you can't see us, we are there for you; we are there for you. Just look at our photographs, just look at our carvings, just look at our imagery, and we'll be there for you. "

NGAHUIA TE AWEKOTUKU, ORGANIZER
OF THE FIRST AUCKLAND GAY DAY

Pride in Asia

The first pride in Asia took place in Tel Aviv, Israel in June 1993. This was followed in the summer of 1994 by Tokyo Pride and the first Pride in Southeast Asia in the Philippines.

Beirut Pride, held in Lebanon in 2017, became the first Pride event held in the Arabic-speaking world.

Pride in South America

South America would host its first official Pride in Buenos Aires in June 1992 called the March of Pride.

A few years later, in 1997, São Paolo would host Brazil's first Pride event which would go on to become one of the largest in the world. The first São Paolo Pride gathered around 2,000 participants, and just ten years later would attract over three million.

Pride in Africa

Africa's first Pride march happened in Johannesburg, South Africa in 1990 and was organized by anti-apartheid activist Simon Nkoli. The first Pride held in Uganda was at its capital, Entebbe, in 2012 as a direct protest against increasingly homophobic laws being introduced in the country, laws which have since culminated in Uganda being the only country in the 21st century to join the list of those that impose the death penalty for same-sex activity.

"I'm fighting for the abolition of apartheid. And I fight for the right of freedom of sexual orientation. These are inextricably linked with each other. I cannot be free as a black man if I am not free as a gay man."

SIMON NKOLI, ORGANIZER OF THE FIRST PRIDE PARADE IN AFRICA

Pride is Everywhere

Amazingly, even Antarctica has a Pride celebration, the first being held on 9 June 2018. This means that every continent has celebrated Pride in one form or another.

Not limited to Earth, NASA astronauts raised a rainbow flag in space aboard the International Space Station in December 2021, taking Pride out of this world.

"Whether it's on the International Space Station or developing the Artemis vehicles that will take us back to the Moon, it's NASA's goal to make space accessible to everyone."

RAJA CHARI, NASA ASTRONAUT, NASA.GOV

EuroPride

The European Pride Organisers Association created EuroPride as a way for Pride to travel across borders. In 1992 the first EuroPride kicked off in London, encouraging LGBTQIA+ Europeans to join together in collective dignity.

Since then it has been staged in many different European cities, including Paris, Warsaw, Riga and Belgrade.

114

> **"Pride is the world's biggest human rights movement, and it is an honor to be part of it. Every Pride event changes lives, and Pride organizations never stop."**
>
> STEVE TAYLOR, EPOA BOARD MEMBER

WorldPride

Rome, Italy, was the host city of the inaugural WorldPride in 2000. Created by InterPride, WorldPride introduces additional events to a city's existing Pride celebration, including an LGBTQIA+ human rights conference to highlight the difficulties experienced by the LGBTQIA+ community. Other host cities include Jerusalem, Toronto and Madrid.

Gathering over five million participants, the 6th celebration of WorldPride was hosted by New York City in 2019 and coincided with the 50th Anniversary of the Stonewall Uprising, becoming the largest LGBTQIA+ event to date.

"It's about shining a light on the work that still needs to be done globally. But also locally, we need to look in our own backyard as well."

KATE WICKETT,
CEO OF SYDNEY WORLDPRIDE,
INTERVIEW IN *ROLLING STONE
AUSTRALIA*, 17 FEBRUARY 2023

> **If gay rights were put in place tomorrow, my behind would still be on fire. I would still be in ultimate danger here, because racism is still in the saddle.**

BARBARA SMITH, SCHOLAR AND ACTIVIST

Black Pride

Looking for a way to bring visibility to the specific issues facing the Black LGBTQIA+ community, the first Black Pride event took place in Washington DC on 25 May 1991.

This event also served as an opportunity to gather the Black LGBTQIA+ community together and promote self-acceptance against homophobia and racism. Its success went on to inspire more Black Pride events around the world.

UK Black Pride

The first UK Black Pride debuted in Southend-on-Sea in 2005 and has become the world's largest celebration for LGBTQIA+ people of African, Asian, Caribbean, Latin American and Middle Eastern-descent.

Due to the cultural diversity of the UK, its mandate expanded beyond the Black community. It is a celebration of unity that uses education, the arts and cultural events to highlight the voices of LGBTQIA+ People of Colour.

" I'm a Black lesbian feminist woman, who is absolutely in support and stands in solidarity with my trans siblings. And if we can all start standing in support with our trans siblings and non-binary siblings we will be better able to turn up the volume on society and make it difficult for them to turn it down on us. "

LADY PHYLL,
CO-FOUNDER OF UK BLACK PRIDE,
INTERVIEW IN *CHERWELL*, 30 JUNE 2023

Violence at Pride

Attending a Pride parade is not always without its dangers. Many parades have been attacked by the police due to systemic homophobia, so their role in parades remains controversial. Some object to the presence of police because of their dubious history relating to LGBTQIA+ rights, while others advocate for their inclusion recognizing LGBTQIA+ police officers and the security they provide to the Pride events.

Pride parades can also be targeted with violence by homophobic members of the public. At the Jerusalem March for Pride and Tolerance in 2015, a 16-year-old Shira Banki was stabbed to death by a religious fanatic. In 2022, Oslo Pride was cancelled on the day it was due to be held following a religiously motivated shooting that targeted the LGBTQIA+ community and killed two people. Many Pride parades across the globe remain on alert for threats of violence.

The Future of Pride

Pride is a demand to be able to live in dignity like anyone else, safe from harm for who you are.

When the LGBTQIA+ community achieves equality in every country, Pride will continue to be commemorated.

More than just a demand for rights, it also honours the memories of the courageous activists and campaigners who fought for their voices to be heard.

Pride continues to inspire people around the world and provides a beacon of hope for those that live in less tolerant societies.

Pride reminds us how far LGBTQIA+ people have come in having the freedom to live their lives how they please, but also how much work still needs to be done in gaining acceptance by society as a whole.

Glossary

The LGBTQIA+ umbrella encompasses a large range of sexualities and gender identities. The plus represents the inclusive nature of the community. This is a non-exhaustive list of definitions of sexualities and gender identities:

Agender   Does not identify with any gender

Aroace   Does not experience romantic or sexual attraction; a combination of aromantic and asexual

Aromantic   Does not experience romantic attraction but may still experience sexual attraction

Asexual   Does not experience sexual attraction but may still experience romantic attraction

Bisexual   Has romantic and sexual attraction to more than one gender (this is inclusive of all genders)

Cisgender   Identifies with the gender they were assigned at birth

Gay   Only has romantic and sexual attraction to someone of the same gender as them, most often used in reference to gay men

Heterosexual   Only has romantic and sexual attraction to the opposite gender

Hijra   Identifies as part of a third gender; this gender identity is exclusive to the Indian subcontinent

Lesbian   A woman who only has romantic and sexual attraction to other women

Non-binary   Does not identify with being a man or a woman, they identify outside of the gender binary of man and woman

Pansexual   Has romantic and sexual attraction to all genders

Polysexual   Has romantic and sexual attraction to more than one gender, but not all genders

Queer   Does not identify as heterosexual or cisgender; this term can encompass a broad range of sexualities and gender identities

Trans man   A transgender person who identifies as a man

Trans woman   A transgender person who identifies as a woman

Transgender   Does not identify with the sex they were assigned at birth

Two-spirit   Takes on attributes of being both male and female, this gender identity is exclusive to Native American culture

"I very much want to inject gay culture into the mainstream. It's not an underground tool for me. It's my whole life."

LADY GAGA,
OUT, SEPTEMBER 2009